This book belongs to:

for Loni

A Busy Week for Salvador

the

Sandhill Crane

Story and Photography by
Margie K. Carroll

Margie Carroll Press
Holly Springs, Georgia

Hello Fr

What a week I've had!
Let me tell you about what happened to me during my first
busy week.

Before I hatched out of my egg, Mom and Dad cared for me.

Mom snuggled over the eggs to keep them warm.
Dad stayed nearby to protect Mom.

For thirty-one days nothing happened.
Then . . .

Early one morning I cracked open my shell and took a look around. Mom was surprised.

Mom and Dad named me Salvador.

Mom cleaned out my eggshell while I explored around the nest.

Two Black-necked Stilts came by.
Mom said they were too nosy for her liking.
She called for Dad.

Dad was sleeping nearby when he heard her call for help.

Dad woke up
and chased the
Stilts away!

Tuesday

I waited for the other egg to hatch.

Mom and I watched and waited.

We all waited and watched, but the other egg never hatched.

I had waited long enough. It was time for fun!

"Not so fast, Salvador," Mom told me.
"You must eat and grow strong."

I played on the nest while Dad and Mom brought me insects and seeds.

Thursday

We took a very long walk.
Mom showed me how to drink
from the shallow puddles in
the marsh.

Sometimes Dad and Mom danced with joy.
They were so proud of me.

Dad fed me tiny crayfish.

Every day I learned new things. Mom and Dad showed me where to find food such as seeds, worms, insects and even lizards.

(I decided to leave the lizards alone until I grew up!)

I learned to stand tall so I could see far away.

I paid very close attention to Mom and Dad.
They said they had a big surprise for Saturday!

Saturday

We went swimming!

There was nothing to it really.

I was a natural.

Sunday

Sunday was the best day of the week!

I got to swim in the deep end of the marsh with Mom and Dad.

Yes, it was a very busy week, I'd say. I hope you had a busy week, too.

Your friend,

Salvador

Notes about Sandhill Cranes

Sandhill Cranes are abundant in the United States numbering about 650,000. They are widely distributed throughout North America. There are three migratory subspecies with breeding ranges in Canada and the northern U.S. The three non-migratory subspecies have restricted ranges including the southern United States and Cuba.

Salvador and his family are members of the Florida non-migratory subspecies. Unlike his cousins of the larger subspecies, the Florida Sandhill Cranes number only about 5,000 and are considered a threatened species. They are protected by the Federal Endangered Species Act.

Florida Sandhill Cranes are long-legged, long-necked, gray birds with a patch of red skin on top of their heads. They fly with their necks outstretched with powerful, rhythmic wing beats and can be 5 ft. tall with wing spans of 6 ft. or more.

Florida's Sandhill Cranes are found in inland shallow freshwater marshes, prairies, pastures and farmlands.

Sandhill Cranes are omnivorous, meaning they eat a variety of plant and animal matter. Some of their favorite meals include seeds, plant tubers, grains, berries, insects, earthworms, mice, snakes, lizards, frogs and crayfish. Unlike other wading birds, such as egrets and herons, Sandhill Cranes do not "fish."

The voice of the Sandhill Crane has been described as a bugling or trumpeting sound. It is one of the most distinctive bird sounds in Florida and can be heard for several miles.

Sandhill Cranes are usually seen in small family groups or pairs. During the winter Florida's Sandhill Crane population increases as cranes from northern states spend the winter in Florida.

Florida Sandhill Cranes stay with the same mate for several years and young sandhills stay with their parents until they are about 10 months old.

Sandhills live to be older than most birds. Some live up to 20 years.

Resource Vocabulary

- beak: the bill of a bird
- chick: the young of any bird
- crane: any of a family of tall wading birds superficially resembling the herons but structurally more nearly related to the rails
- crayfish: any of numerous freshwater decapod crustaceans resembling the lobster but usually much smaller
- endangered: a species whose numbers are so small that the species is at risk of extinction
- environment: the circumstances, objects or conditions by which one is surrounded
- erosion: a gradual decline of something
- feathers: any of the light horny epidermal outgrowths that form the external covering of the body of birds and that consist of a shaft bearing on each side a series of barbs
- habitat: a place where an animal naturally lives or a plant naturally grows
- marsh: a tract of soft wet land usually characterized with grasses, sedge or cattails
- migrate: to pass usually periodically from one region or climate to another for feeding or breeding
- molt: to shed hair, feathers, shell, horns or an outer layer periodically
- nest: where birds lay their eggs and hatch their young
- offspring: a child or animal as related to its parent
- omnivorous: feeding on both animal and vegetable substances
- plumage: the feathers of a bird
- pollution: undesirable state of the natural environment being contaminated with harmful substances as a consequence of human activities
- protection: something that keeps (one) safe
- swamp: a wet area that is normally covered by water all year and is not subject to drying out during the summer
- wetlands: a general term applied to open-water habitats and seasonally or permanently waterlogged land areas, including lakes, rivers, estuarine and freshwater marshes

Questions for Young Readers

What kind of bird is Salvador?	Sandhill Crane
Is he cared for by both parents?	Yes
Was he born in a nest?	Yes
Could he walk right after he hatched?	Yes
Was he left alone by his parents?	No, they stayed with him.
Did Salvador live in the desert?	No, he lived in a marsh/wetland.
What nosy neighbors bothered Salvador's Mom?	Black-necked Stilts
How did Salvador's father protect him?	He chased the Stilts away.
What did the father feed Salvador?	Crayfish, insects, seeds, worms
Did the parents give Salvador water?	No, they taught him how to drink.

Salvador and his family are members of the Florida Sandhill Crane subspecies. These images were taken near Englewood, Florida.

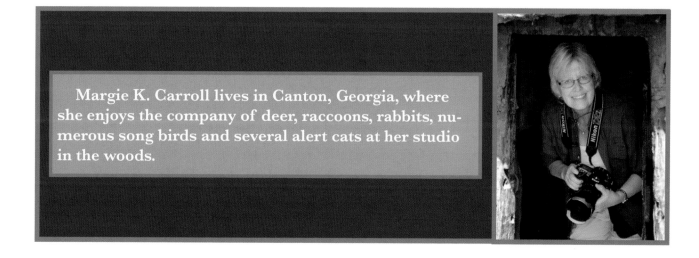

Margie K. Carroll lives in Canton, Georgia, where she enjoys the company of deer, raccoons, rabbits, numerous song birds and several alert cats at her studio in the woods.

Special thanks to Esther, Doris, Carol and Linda.

Margie K. Carroll
email: coalcat@mac.com
678-488-5183
www.margiecarrollpress.com

OurRainbow Press Marietta, GA
Printed in Atlanta, GA

Margie Carroll Press
P.O Box 581
Holly Springs, GA 30142